P9-CBA-783

WORLD WAR II LEADERS

WORLD WAR II LEADERS

ESSENTIAL LIBRARY OF WORLD WAR II

Essential Library

An Imprint of Abdo Publishing
abdopublishing.com

BY RUSSELL ROBERTS

CONTENT CONSULTANT

ALLAN M. WINKLER
PROFESSOR OF HISTORY
MIAMI UNIVERSITY

abdopublishing.com

Printed in the United States of America, North Mankato, Minnesota

052015
092015

Cover Photos: AP Images (left); Bettmann/Corbis (right)

Interior Photos: AP Images, 1 (left), 3 (left), 16 (top), 16 (left), 16 (middle), 16 (right), 17 (middle), 18, 21, 22, 24, 28, 35, 39, 44, 53, 57, 63, 67, 70, 73, 86, 87, 90, 93, 95, 97, 98 (bottom), 99 (left), 99 (right); Bettmann/Corbis, 1 (right), 3 (right), 17 (top), 31, 65, 83; Hugo Jaeger/Timepix/The LIFE Picture Collection/Getty Images, 6, 98 (top); Keystone/Getty Images, 9; Leslie Priest/AP Images, 11; Yevgeny Khaldei/ITAR-TASS/AP Images, 15; APIC/Getty Images, 17 (bottom), 60, 80; British Official Photo/AP Images, 36, 55; Berliner Verlag/Archiv/Picture-Alliance/DPA/AP Images, 40, 77; Heinrich Hoffmann/EPA/Corbis, 49; CAF pap/AP Images, 47; Hulton-Deutsch Collection/Corbis, 50; US National Archives and Records Administration, 79

Editor: Arnold Ringstad
Series Designers: Kelsey Oseid and Maggie Villaume

Library of Congress Control Number: 2015931285

Cataloging-in-Publication Data

Roberts, Russell.
World War II leaders / Russell Roberts.
p. cm. -- (Essential library of World War II)
Includes bibliographical references and index.
ISBN 978-1-62403-798-6
1. Military leadership--Juvenile literature. 2. Generals--Juvenile literature. 3. World War, 1939-1945--Juvenile literature. I. Title.
940.53--dc23

2015931285

CONTENTS

Hitler later gave speeches at the Munich beer hall to commemorate the events of November 1923.

THE WORLD IN FLAMES

Bullets flew all around Adolf Hitler, knocking several of his companions to the ground. He dove for cover as the bullets whizzed past, injuring his shoulder as he hit the hard pavement. He looked around at his companions bleeding and dying around him. It was November 9, 1923, on the streets of Munich, Germany.

Only the day before, local official Gustav von Kahr had been speaking to a crowd of 3,000 businessmen in Munich's Burgerbraukeller, or Citizen's Beer Hall. As Kahr spoke, Hitler, dressed in formal clothing, led a group of 25 men into the beer hall from the back entrance.[1] Suddenly Hitler rushed toward the stage. His men lined up along the wall. Their purpose was obvious: nobody was leaving.

Hitler fired a revolver into the air. "The national revolution is begun!" he shouted.[2] The hall erupted into a panic. Some in the crowd recognized Hitler. He was the leader of the National Socialist

German Workers Party (NSDAP), sometimes referred to as the Nazi Party. Others did not know him at all.

Hitler hustled Kahr into a back room. He soon returned to the stage. The beer hall was an excited babble of voices. Hitler fired his pistol again to quiet the crowd. He proclaimed Kahr had agreed to support him in his takeover of the German government. He also said the national government in Berlin had been overthrown. As Hitler spoke, his words seemed to some observers to cast a spell over the audience. One witness recalled: "In a few sentences he totally transformed the mood of the audience. I have rarely experienced anything like it."[3]

At the end of the evening, everyone in the beer hall was allowed to leave, including Kahr. He quickly contacted the national government in Berlin, which had not been overthrown, and told them what had happened.

The next day, on November 9, Hitler and approximately 2,000 of his followers went to take over the nearby Bavarian Defense Ministry.[4] They had not gone very far, however, when they came upon a large group of police blocking their way. Kahr's phone call had raised the alarm.

Suddenly a shot rang out. The police fired a storm of bullets into the crowd. As people started falling all around him, Hitler dove to the ground, dislocating his shoulder. He crawled to a waiting car, threw himself in, and was driven away. Behind him 16 Nazis lay dead on the street.[5] The attempted coup, later called the Beer Hall Putsch, had failed. Hitler was arrested, found guilty of treason, and sentenced to five years in prison. Many Germans thought they had seen the last of him. They were wrong.

Nazis would brutally murder Kahr ten years later as revenge for his actions during the attempted takeover.

A POWDER KEG WORLD

By 1939, global politics was chaotic. It was akin to a powder keg with several slowly burning fuses attached. At any moment, one of these fuses could cause it to explode into war. The leaders of the world's most powerful nations saw a new world war on the horizon.

One contributing factor to the war was the Treaty of Versailles, which had ended World War I (1914–1918). This treaty had harshly punished Germany for its role in the war, barring it from building up another strong military. Historian A. J. P. Taylor later noted that the treaty's weakness was that it did not include any way for its provisions to be enforced. Instead, it relied on German cooperation. Once Hitler became the leader of Germany in 1933, that cooperation stopped.

Hitler, with his vision of Lebensraum, or "living space," for Germany, tried to build a massive German empire. In March 1938, he annexed neighboring Austria.

TREATY OF VERSAILLES

Some historians believe the Treaty of Versailles, which ended World War I, was a major contributing factor to World War II. Among its provisions was the removal of German territories, including the port city of Danzig and the area of Alsace Lorraine. It also cut the German army to 100,000 soldiers, reduced the German navy to 36 ships and no submarines, and banned Germany from possessing an air force.[6] The treaty required Germany to accept total blame for the war and to pay large sums of money in reparations. German public opinion was against the treaty. Political groups, including the fascist, nationalist Nazis, rose to prominence by denouncing the treaty.

Large crowds greeted Chamberlain upon his return to the United Kingdom.

He then threatened Czechoslovakia. Many ethnic Germans lived in a section of Czechoslovakia known as the Sudetenland, and Hitler wanted to seize this land for Germany. Desperate to avoid war, British and French officials met with him in Munich at the end of September and agreed he could take the Sudetenland. No Czechoslovakian representatives were present. Hitler claimed this would be his final territorial request. When British prime minister Neville Chamberlain returned home, he said, "I believe [the Munich Agreement] is peace for our time."[7] This peace ended up lasting less than a year. On September 1, 1939, Germany invaded Poland, beginning World War II.

THE WORLD AT WAR

In response to the invasion of Poland, France and the United Kingdom declared war on Germany on September 3, 1939. Two weeks later, thanks to a secret portion of a nonaggression pact between the Soviet Union and Germany, the Soviets invaded Poland.

Initially the war went well for Germany. Hitler unleashed his blitzkrieg, or lightning war, against the Poles, who could do little against the massed German tanks and planes. Warsaw, the Polish capital, surrendered on September 27. Germany and the Soviet Union, led by Joseph Stalin, divided the conquered country between them.

After several months of little activity, a period known as the "Phony War," Germany sprang to life in the spring of 1940 and invaded Norway, Denmark, Belgium, Holland, and France. Several of the defenders, including French commander Charles De Gaulle, put up

BLITZKRIEG

The key to the German army's early success in World War II was blitzkrieg, and the key to blitzkrieg was speed. The idea behind blitzkrieg was to use fast, mechanized vehicles to race through the front lines and attack the enemy's rear areas, where vital communication and supply links could be disrupted. Then the main body of troops would sweep through and attack what was left—often a confused and disorganized mass of soldiers. Germany's opponents were unprepared for blitzkrieg, leading to early German successes during the war.

a strong resistance, but they all fell to Germany. Chamberlain, who had sadly misjudged Hitler, resigned his position on May 10, 1940. Winston Churchill replaced him as the United Kingdom's prime minister. Churchill assumed control of a nation that now stood alone against the Nazis.

From mid-July through the end of October, the German air force, the Luftwaffe, bombed the United Kingdom. Germany hoped to pave the way for a land invasion. But the British Royal Air Force (RAF) fought back fiercely, preventing Germany from controlling the skies over the United Kingdom. The invasion never occurred.

On September 22, 1940, Germany, Italy, and Japan entered into an alliance with the signing of the Tripartite Pact. The three countries became known as the Axis powers. On June 22, 1941, Hitler launched Operation Barbarossa, a surprise invasion of the Soviet Union. The Soviet Union immediately switched to the British side and fought back.

On December 7, 1941, Japan attacked the US military base at Pearl Harbor, Hawaii. More than 2,000 Americans died. Pressured by his nation's powerful military, Japanese emperor Hirohito had approved the attack. The United States had been technically neutral, though it had been supplying the United Kingdom with aid. After Pearl Harbor, US president Franklin D. Roosevelt asked the US Congress to declare war on Japan. It did so immediately. Several days later, Japan's ally, Germany, declared war on the United States. The United States was now at war on two continents. The United States, the Soviet Union, and the United Kingdom were known as the Allies.

THE SAME BOAT

Winston Churchill heard about the Japanese attack on Pearl Harbor while he was at dinner. Churchill left his dinner, and some of his aides were afraid that he was going to declare war on Japan. In fact, Churchill went to call Franklin D. Roosevelt, the president of the United States, to ask if the reports were true. Roosevelt came onto the line and said, "It's quite true . . . we're all in the same boat now."[8]

After Japan's initial successes in the Pacific, the United States defeated it at the Battle of Midway in June 1942. The tide of the Pacific war began turning. Meanwhile, Germany's invasion of Russia had stalled. The British won significant battles against the Italians and Germans in North Africa.

Axis forces suffered further losses in 1943. The Allies landed in southern Italy in mid-June and began surging north. The Soviets began pushing the Germans out of their country in July. Italian dictator Benito Mussolini was overthrown and imprisoned in July 1943, although German soldiers rescued him from his mountaintop prison. But Italy was effectively out of the war. In the Pacific, US forces gained steadily against the Japanese.

On June 6, 1944, the Allies launched an invasion of German-occupied France. By the end of the year, both Rome, Italy, and Paris, France, had been freed from Nazi control. De Gaulle returned from exile to command French forces on the continent. Germany made a final, desperate offensive thrust in December. Its failure left the road to Berlin, the German capital, wide open.

In April 1945, US and Soviet forces began the final push to Berlin. The city was a smoking ruin following months of brutal warfare. There was no electricity, gas, or sanitation. Little food was available, and fire hydrants supplied the only available water. In early May, Germany surrendered. After taking back a series of Japanese-controlled islands in the Pacific, the United States dropped atomic bombs on Hiroshima and Nagasaki in August, and Japan also surrendered. After six long years, the war was over. Some of the warring nations' leaders had survived to see the end of the conflict. Others had not been so lucky.

World War II came to an end in Europe as Soviet soldiers hoisted their flag over the ruins of Berlin.

LEADERS
AND THEIR COUNTRIES

WINSTON CHURCHILL
UNITED KINGDOM

FRANKLIN D. ROOSEVELT
UNITED STATES

CHARLES DE GAULLE
FRANCE

BENITO MUSSOLINI
ITALY

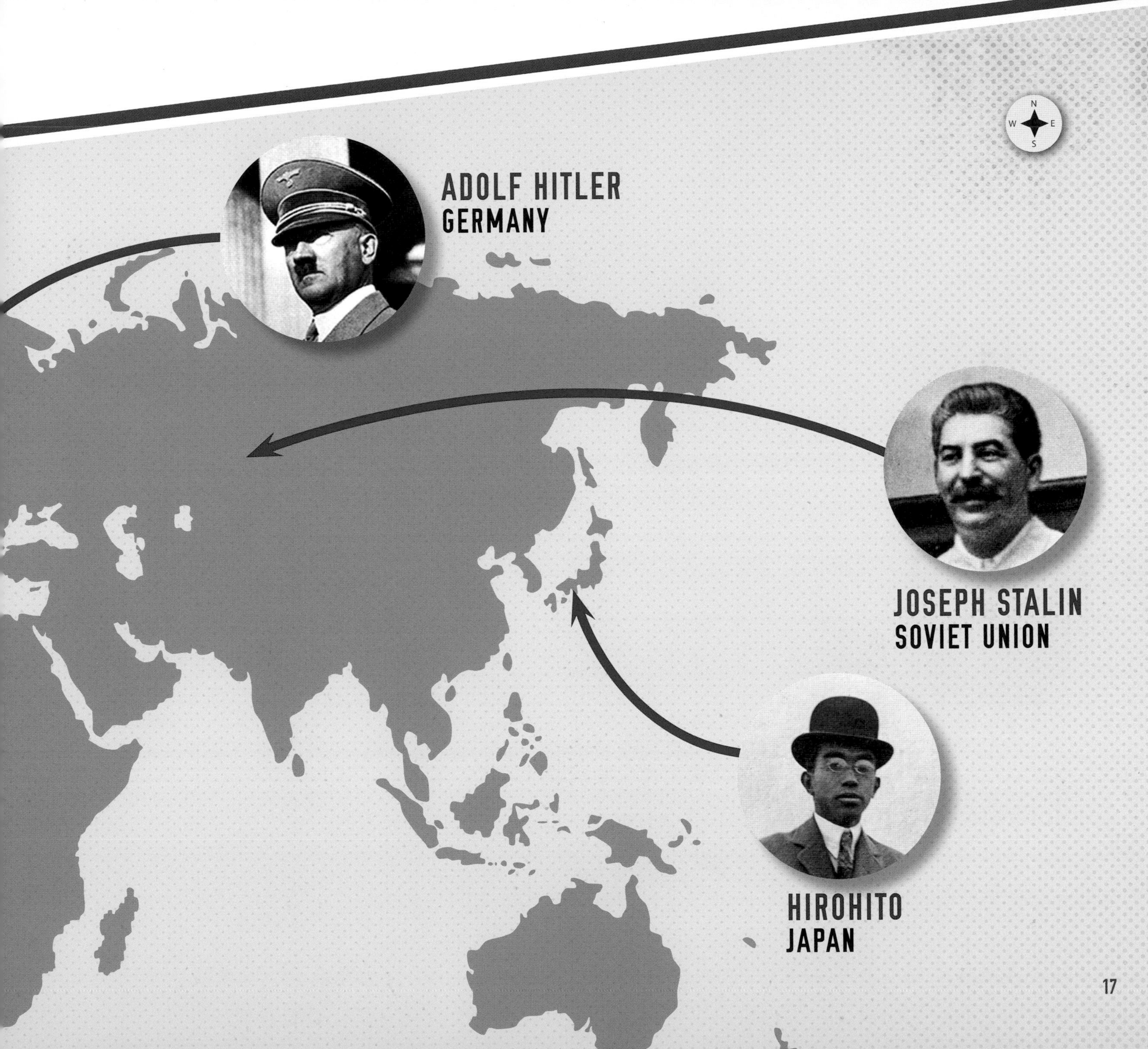
N
W
E
S
ADOLF HITLER
GERMANY
JOSEPH STALIN
SOVIET UNION
HIROHITO
JAPAN

Roosevelt served as assistant secretary of the navy during World War I.

FRANKLIN D. ROOSEVELT

Franklin D. Roosevelt was the president of the United States during nearly all of World War II. Roosevelt was born on January 30, 1882, in Hyde Park, New York. His wealthy family was a well-known force in American politics. His distant cousin Theodore Roosevelt had been the president of the United States from 1901 to 1909. He married Eleanor Roosevelt, one of Theodore Roosevelt's nieces, in 1905. Roosevelt rose through the ranks of the Democratic Party, becoming a member of the New York State Senate and serving as assistant secretary of the navy.

In 1921, Roosevelt was stricken with the disease polio, paralyzing him from the waist down. The disease seemed as though it might end his promising political career. However, Roosevelt continued to be active in politics. He remained a popular figure, winning the election for governor of New York in 1928.

By 1932, the United States was in the grip of the major economic downturn known as the Great Depression. Millions were unemployed and desperate for change. Proclaiming he would turn the country's fortunes around, Roosevelt swept to victory in the 1932 presidential election. His economic recovery program, known as the New Deal, made sweeping changes in an attempt to pull the country out of depression. In 1936, he won an easy reelection to a second term.

FIRE IN THE NEIGHBOR'S HOUSE

After his reelection, as the world slid slowly toward war, Roosevelt thought he could keep the United States out of the conflict. He envisioned the country as an "arsenal of democracy," providing the United Kingdom with weapons and support but not becoming involved in actual combat.[1] In a series of radio broadcasts called fireside chats, he told the US public about his plans for improving the domestic economy and dealing with foreign affairs.

In the Pacific, Roosevelt viewed Japan's expansion warily. Japan had invaded China in the 1930s and was setting up its own empire. There had not been any direct conflict between the United States and Japan, but some warned of Japan's true intentions. Joseph Grew, the US ambassador to Japan, relayed information he had received from a Peruvian official: "There is a lot of talk . . . that the Japanese, in case of a break with the United States, are planning . . . a surprise mass attack on Pearl Harbor."[2]

ELEANOR ROOSEVELT

1884–1962

Eleanor Roosevelt was the wife of President Franklin D. Roosevelt and served as First Lady during his entire presidential tenure. Born in New York City on October 11, 1884, Eleanor was a niece of President Theodore Roosevelt. He gave her away to Franklin at the couple's wedding on March 17, 1905.

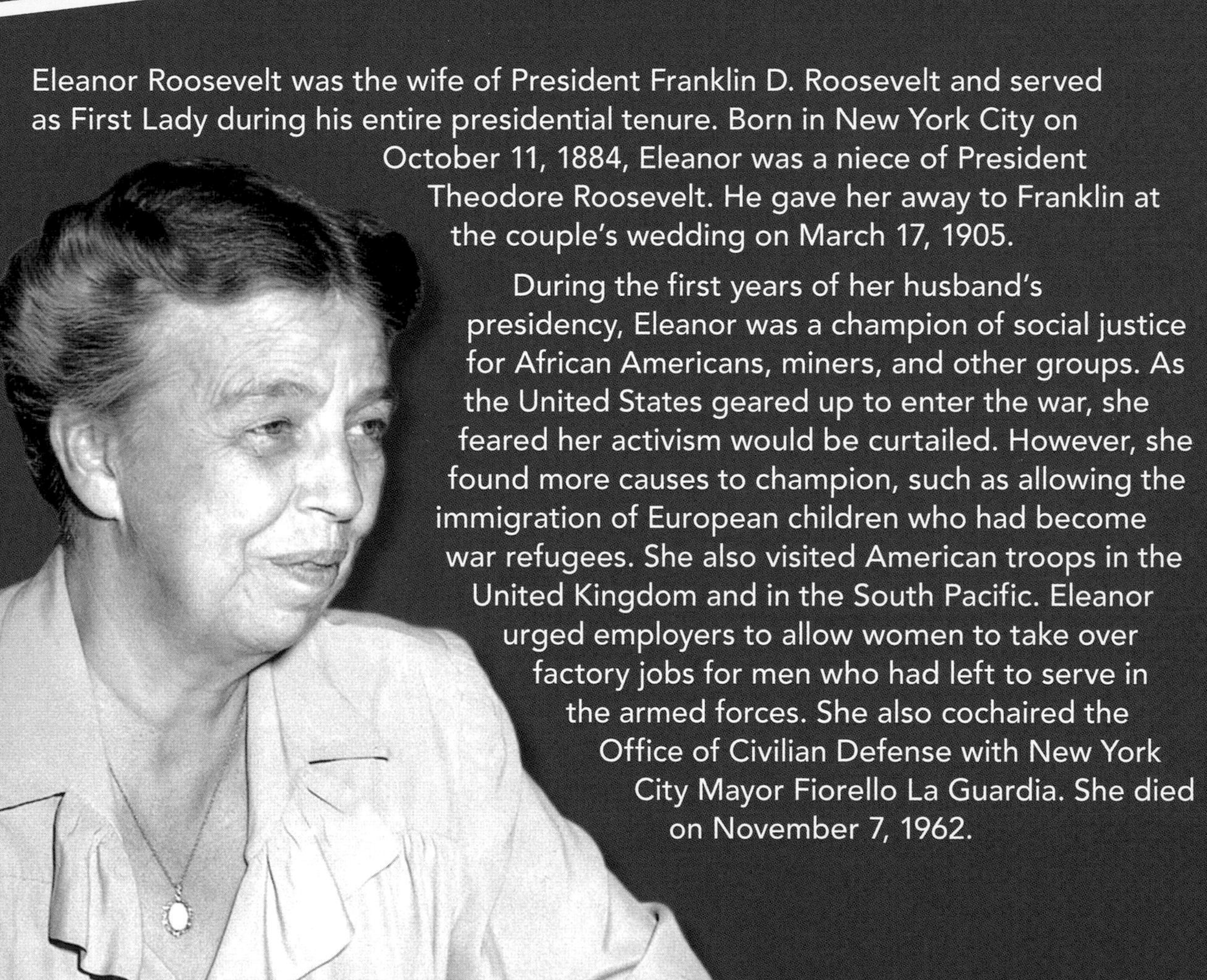

During the first years of her husband's presidency, Eleanor was a champion of social justice for African Americans, miners, and other groups. As the United States geared up to enter the war, she feared her activism would be curtailed. However, she found more causes to champion, such as allowing the immigration of European children who had become war refugees. She also visited American troops in the United Kingdom and in the South Pacific. Eleanor urged employers to allow women to take over factory jobs for men who had left to serve in the armed forces. She also cochaired the Office of Civilian Defense with New York City Mayor Fiorello La Guardia. She died on November 7, 1962.

Roosevelt's fireside chats made him a popular and trusted figure.

In December 1940, a month after his election to a third term as president, Roosevelt unveiled the Lend-Lease program. Under the program, the United States loaned the United Kingdom the war material it needed with the understanding it would return the material when the war was over. The president compared the program to loaning a neighbor a garden hose to extinguish the fire in his burning house.

During the first years of the war, many Americans were strongly against their nation entering the war. Known as isolationists, some formed the America First group. Among its prominent members were automaker Henry Ford and famed aviator Charles Lindbergh. The movement's popularity meant Roosevelt had to carefully straddle the line between helping the United Kingdom and keeping the country from entering an outright war.

Hitler, aware of the potential industrial and military strength of the United States, tried to avoid provoking the United States into the war. He hoped the European war would end before the United States had a chance to enter the fighting. However, Germany's surprise invasion of the Soviet Union on June 22, 1941, helped push Roosevelt closer to war. Suddenly the Soviets needed equipment to fight against the Nazis, just as the United Kingdom did. A steady stream of US weapons and vehicles began entering the Soviet Union. Still, the United States was not officially at war.

AFRICAN AMERICANS IN DEFENSE INDUSTRIES

Early in the war, racist attitudes in the war industries prevented African Americans from getting hired for jobs to build US weapons and equipment. African-American union head A. Philip Randolph planned a huge march on Washington to protest this discrimination. Fearful of violence occurring if the march took place, Roosevelt signed Executive Order 8802 on June 25, 1941. It banned discrimination in defense industries and government based on race, religion, or national origin. The order resulted in employment for thousands of African Americans who made vital contributions to the war effort.

GOING TO WAR

On December 7, 1941, the Japanese suddenly attacked the US naval base at

The United States officially declared war on Japan just hours after Roosevelt's request.

Pearl Harbor, Hawaii. The next day, calling December 7 a "date which will live in infamy," Roosevelt asked the US Congress to declare war on Japan.[3] A few days later, both Germany and Italy declared war on the United States.

Some historians accuse Roosevelt of ignoring warnings about a potential Pearl Harbor attack so he could use it as an excuse for entering the war. Others have noted that Roosevelt's background as assistant secretary of the navy meant he would be unlikely to allow US ships to be destroyed.

Once Pearl Harbor brought the United States into the war, Roosevelt became a central member of the Allies. He said, "I am responsible for keeping the grand alliance together."[4]

Roosevelt was being pulled in two different directions in the overall war strategy. Some wanted the United States to concentrate its efforts against Japan first. Others thought Germany posed the greater threat and advocated focusing on the Nazis. Roosevelt agreed, believing Germany had to be beaten before Japan so the Soviet Union could be relieved. He stuck to this guiding principle throughout the war. Still, US forces were engaged in a two-front war, with relatively small numbers of US Marines invading islands in the Pacific while the much larger US Army fought in Europe.

Roosevelt and Churchill, as leaders of democracies, got along well together. But Stalin's Soviet Union was very different from the United States and the United Kingdom. Stalin ruled his nation as a harsh dictator, suppressing opposing points of view and persecuting those who acted against him. Nevertheless, Roosevelt felt he could handle Stalin. He said of Stalin:

JAPANESE-AMERICAN INTERNMENT

After Pearl Harbor, people of Japanese ancestry living in the United States found themselves under suspicion by their fellow Americans. Political pressure mounted on Roosevelt to do something. On February 19, 1942, Roosevelt signed Executive Order 9066. It enabled the military to remove Japanese Americans from their homes and confine them to internment camps. Many thousands of Japanese Americans lost their homes, had their lives severely disrupted, and were labeled disloyal. Historians harshly criticized Roosevelt for signing the order. The US government officially apologized for the internment in 1988.

"I think if I give him everything I possibly can, and ask nothing from him in return . . . he won't try to annex anything and will work with me for a world of peace and democracy."[5]

THE NEW WORLD ORDER

Together, Roosevelt, Churchill, and Stalin were known as the Big Three. The trio held two face-to-face conferences during the war. The first was at Tehran, Iran, in November 1943, and the second was at Yalta, in the Soviet Union, in February 1945. At these conferences they made critical strategic decisions about the war. They also discussed how the postwar world would look.

Roosevelt's vision beyond the war was a new world order without colonial empires. Roosevelt wanted the Allies to act as the policemen of the world, keeping peace with their armed forces and preventing other nations from secretly rearming themselves, as Germany had done under Hitler. He avoided discussing this with Churchill, since the United Kingdom itself had a colonial empire and it would seem as if he was against his ally.

AN ILL MAN

Roosevelt ran for a fourth term as president in 1944. Although both Germany and Japan were in retreat, the war was not yet over, and he wanted to see it through. His campaign against Republican challenger Thomas E. Dewey emphasized his experience as a wartime commander. But Roosevelt's health had been deteriorating. He was diagnosed with acute bronchitis, heart disease, and high blood pressure.

YALTA

Roosevelt's actions at Yalta in February 1945 later came under severe criticism. He was blamed for allowing Stalin to establish control over Eastern and Central European countries after the war. Others note that the failure of Roosevelt and Churchill to open a second front in Western Europe in order to take pressure off of the Soviet Union in the East gave Stalin additional bargaining power. The Soviet Union fought Germany alone in Europe until the Allied invasion of France in June 1944. This large contribution to the war effort may have given Stalin additional prestige and power at Yalta, enabling him to make additional claims in postwar Europe.

Roosevelt's main priority at Yalta was to secure a promise from Stalin that the Soviet Union would join the fight against Japan once Germany was defeated. Stalin agreed, and he held to his commitment, declaring war on Japan in August 1945. No one knew how long and difficult the struggle against Japan would be, and Roosevelt wanted all the help he could get.

Despite his health, Roosevelt won his fourth term as president in November 1944. Tired and ill, Roosevelt decided against a big inaugural parade to celebrate the victory. Instead, he held the January 1945 ceremony on a White House balcony, followed by a small reception with a few guests. A few days later, he left for Yalta to meet with Stalin and Churchill.

By the end of March 1945, now back in Washington, DC, Roosevelt was exhausted from the strenuous Yalta trip. He decided to go to his vacation retreat at Warm Springs, Georgia. There he hoped the pine tree–lined resort near a refreshing hot spring would rejuvenate him, as it had done so many times before.

Mussolini, *center*, gained tens of thousands of fascist followers in the early 1920s.

BENITO MUSSOLINI

Benito Mussolini was the prime minister of Italy during World War II. He aligned Italy with Germany and Japan as a member of the Axis powers. Mussolini was born on July 29, 1883, in the Italian town of Dovia di Predappio. He took an interest in politics, becoming a journalist and a socialist early in life. Around 1919 he developed a political philosophy called fascism, which placed the power of the nation above that of the individual.

THE BLACKSHIRTS

The fascist movement in Italy grew rapidly in the early 1920s. It was led by the Blackshirts, an armed organization loyal to Mussolini. Fascist takeovers occurred in Milan and other places throughout Italy. The advisers of Italian king Victor Emmanuel III recommended he put Mussolini in control of the government to end the chaos. On October 31, 1922, Mussolini was sworn in as Italy's prime minister.

Mussolini's goal was not just to lead Italy but to become its dictator. He eliminated prominent opponents, including politicians and newspaper editors. By the end of 1925, Mussolini had brought the Italian Parliament, the nation's courts, and the governmental bureaucracy all under his control. He was known in Italy as Il Duce, or "the leader."

KING VICTOR EMMANUEL III

Victor Emmanuel was born in Naples, Italy, on November 11, 1869. He became king of Italy in 1900, following the assassination of his father, Umberto. In the early 1920s, Italy was caught between socialists and the fascists led by Mussolini. On October 28, 1922, in a bid to end the struggle and restore law and order, Victor Emmanuel asked Mussolini to form a government. Mussolini became prime minister of Italy and soon turned it into a dictatorship that did not end until his removal in 1943. Victor Emanuel gave up the throne in 1946, and the Italian monarchy ended a few weeks later.

FOREIGN POLICY

Mussolini's foreign policy emphasized expansion. He believed Italy's growing population meant the nation needed a colonial empire. He felt it was necessary for Italy to become a world power. A successful war, Mussolini believed, would enable Italy to assume a dominant role among nations and promote fascist ideas. "The more enemies the greater the honor," Mussolini said.[1]

On October 2, 1935, bells and sirens brought the Italian people to town squares to learn that Italy had begun a war against Ethiopia in East Africa. Ethiopia's military was much weaker than Italy's. Its soldiers were poorly trained and equipped with

The people of conquered Ethiopia were forced to praise Mussolini.

weapons dating to World War I or even earlier. Many had no firearms at all. The war ended in May 1936, when Italian forces occupied Addis Ababa, Ethiopia's capital. Ethiopia became a part of Italian East Africa. As the Italian people read of the success of the Italian military, Mussolini's popularity rose.

Mussolini's next move was involving Italy in the Spanish Civil War (1936–1939). He wanted a fascist victory in Spain so that the country would align with him against the British. Mussolini anticipated a quick victory by Spanish leader Francisco Franco, but as the war dragged on, the Italian dictator was forced to continue sending troops and material. By the time Franco finally triumphed in March 1939, it had cost Italy more than 15,000 casualties.[2]

MAKING THE TRAINS RUN ON TIME

Italy's fascists used the expression "Mussolini made the trains run on time" as a way to justify the fascist government. The thinking went that it may have been a dictatorship, but at least it got things done. This effectiveness was supposedly demonstrated by getting the trains to run on schedule. However, this was a myth spread by fascist propagandists. In reality, the government banned all reporting of train accidents or delays, so it gave the appearance of the trains always running on time even when they did not.

THE CULT OF PERSONALITY

Mussolini established a cult of personality around himself. People were encouraged to worship him as a strong, effective, perfect leader of the Italian people. Part of his image was that of a super sportsman. The Italian people were told a typical day for him included horseback riding, fencing, and possibly swimming.

He was reported to have worked at least 18 hours per day, and it was claimed he could even work night after night with no sleep. He supposedly attended 25 meetings per day. His propaganda suggested he devised a precise plan dictating every one of his actions for the following year. However, it was also said he could instantly act on his instincts, which were never wrong.

The Italian people were flooded with photographs of Mussolini in heroic poses. An estimated 30 million photos of Mussolini were in circulation, prompting some observers to call him the most photographed man in history.[3]

ALLIANCE WITH GERMANY

Italy's involvement in the Spanish Civil War brought it closer to Germany, which was also helping Franco. Mussolini did not want to align with either France or the United Kingdom. He felt Italy and Germany had a "common destiny."[4] Mussolini repeatedly swore to Hitler that Italy was ready to fight alongside Germany.

THE SPANISH CIVIL WAR

As other nations moved toward a world war in the late 1930s, one European nation was experiencing violence within its own borders. The Spanish Civil War pitted the forces of Spain's government, known as the Republicans, against the fascist rebels, known as the Nationalists. General Francisco Franco led the Nationalists. Both sides received outside help. The Nationalists were aided by Germany and Italy, who used the war as a testing ground for the type of tank and air warfare they would use in World War II. The Soviet Union, as well as small groups of antifascist fighters from foreign nations, supported the Republicans. Ultimately the Nationalists won. Franco remained dictator of Spain until his death in 1975.

On May 7, 1939, Italy and Germany signed an alliance known as the Pact of Steel, making the two countries military allies. A few weeks later, Mussolini wrote to Hitler that although he considered war a foregone conclusion, he wanted it postponed until the end of 1942 so that Italy would be ready. Ignoring his request, Hitler launched the invasion of Poland in 1939, beginning World War II. Mussolini responded that because of Hitler's "treachery," Italy would not enter the fight.[5]

MUSSOLINI AND HITLER

At first Hitler was a great admirer of Mussolini. His attempted overthrow of the German government in the Beer Hall Putsch in 1923 was an attempt to copy Mussolini's 1922 March on Rome. After Hitler came to power, fascist ideology brought the two countries closer together. In private, Mussolini found Hitler long-winded. He expressed scorn when Hitler spoke of the superiority of the German race, believing that it was the Italians who were superior. When war broke out, German military successes relegated Mussolini to a junior partner in the relationship.

LOSING THE WAR

By June 1940, German victories in Western Europe made it seem the war might end with no involvement from Italy at all. However, Mussolini finally declared war on France and the United Kingdom on June 10, 1940. "We go into the field against the . . . democracies of the West, who . . . have threatened the existence of the Italian people," he said.[6]

Before declaring war, advisers warned Mussolini that Italy was not prepared for anything other than a brief campaign. The Italian army soon proved them right. Though it won minor successes in East Africa, it suffered severe losses in North

Africa and Greece throughout 1941 and 1942.

As the military situation worsened in January 1943, Mussolini appeared ready to collapse. He could barely leave his bed, and the government seemed as if it had ceased to function. The regime had another setback in March and April 1943, when Italian workers went on strike. The country was swept by the feeling that further fighting was useless. Mussolini seemed divorced from reality, speaking publicly about food supplies being abundant while at the same time Italians were dying of hunger. He also claimed to have a mysterious secret weapon he would soon unleash.

On July 10, 1943, the Allies landed in Sicily and soon seized the island. Mussolini promised his special defense plans would throw the invaders back

Mussolini made frequent public appearances with Hitler, linking himself to the more powerful dictator.

The movement of Allied tanks into North Africa in early 1943 signaled the coming of the end of Mussolini's overseas empire.

into the sea, but no such plans existed. Rome was bombed for the first time on July 19.

On July 24, Italy's Grand Council of Fascism met and voted to remove Mussolini from power. Among those who voted against him was Galeazzo Ciano, one of his top officials. Ignoring the vote, Mussolini worked the next day as usual. Later that day Mussolini met with King Victor Emmanuel. To his shock, the king told him he was being replaced as prime minister. Mussolini was arrested and taken away.

GALEAZZO CIANO

Gian Galeazzo Ciano was born on March 18, 1903, in Lovorno, Italy. In 1930, he married Mussolini's daughter, becoming the dictator's son-in-law. In 1935, he was named minister of press and propaganda, and the following year he became Italy's foreign minister. Ciano knew the Italian military was unprepared for a major war, and as World War II turned against Italy, he urged that the country withdraw from the conflict. He eventually voted to remove Mussolini from power in July 1943. Surviving fascist forces executed Ciano for treason on January 11, 1944. He left behind an extensive diary that has given historians a close look at the inner workings of the Axis powers.

A DARING RESCUE

After Mussolini was stripped of power and arrested in July 1943, he was sent to a penal colony on the Italian island of Ponza. He was later imprisoned at the Campo Imperatore Hotel, a ski resort high in the Apennine Mountains. However, unknown to Mussolini, he was the subject of a prison breakout scheme ordered by Hitler. Hitler had personally selected the man in charge of the mission, Otto Skornezy.

Using intercepted intelligence, Skornezy traced Mussolini to his hotel prison. On September 12, 1943, Skornezy and a team of commandos landed gliders on the mountain, then overwhelmed the Italian security forces guarding Mussolini without a shot being fired. The German team, along with Mussolini, fled in light planes.

Three days later, Mussolini was reunited with Hitler. With Nazi backing, Mussolini set up a new government in the town of Salo. His new country, called the Italian Social Republic, was established on September 23, 1943. In reality, the new country controlled only the northern section of Italy and could not exist without German support.

German commandos evacuated Mussolini to Axis-controlled territory.

Hitler, *left*, and other Nazi officials were imprisoned for their role in the attempted 1923 coup.

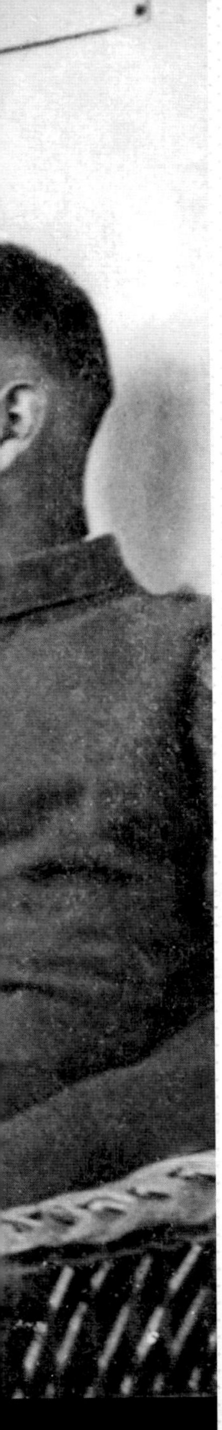

ADOLF HITLER

The man who led Nazi Germany and was responsible for starting World War II was born on April 20, 1889, in Braunau am Inn, Austria-Hungary. After serving in the German military during World War I, Hitler became head of the German Workers Party, a forerunner of the Nazi Party, in 1921. In 1923, he tried to seize power in a Munich beer hall. The coup failed, and Hitler spent the next nine months in prison, where he wrote his book *Mein Kampf*, or "My Struggle."

After his release, he concentrated on taking power legally, growing the party, and making fiery speeches denouncing the Treaty of Versailles. By 1933, the Nazis were the largest elected party in Germany. That year, Hitler was named chancellor of Germany by president Paul von Hindenburg. When Hindenburg died the following year, Hitler also assumed the presidency. As had

Mussolini, he quickly turned his rule into a dictatorship. Hitler took the title führer, or leader.

GERMAN EXPANSION

Hitler's driving political force was to restore a sense of German national greatness that was lost following the nation's defeat in World War I. He believed this could be accomplished only by war. Hitler tied this renewal of German greatness with his concept of Lebensraum, which meant that Germany needed more land for expansion. Lebensraum was not a new idea in Germany. German geographer Friedrich Ratzel had developed the concept in the 1800s. Hitler read Ratzel's work during his imprisonment, and he discussed its ideas with fellow prisoners.

At one point early in his political career, Hitler was convinced France was Germany's greatest enemy, and he once even proposed an alliance with the Soviet Union. However, by the time he wrote *Mein Kampf*, that view had changed. Hitler said Lebensraum must come from the Soviet Union in the east. Fate, he said, had selected Germany to conquer this territory.

Members of the German business community agreed with Hitler's idea of living space, since it meant new sources of raw materials. The military, still

MEIN KAMPF

Rarely does a dictator lay out his plan for world domination in a book written years before it happens. But Hitler did just that in *Mein Kampf*. In the book, Hitler describes his plan for living space, and how it has to come from the east—specifically, the Soviet Union. Hitler writes of his hatred of Jews. His feelings about the Jews foreshadow the murder of some 6 million Jewish people during the Holocaust. He also discusses the political program the Nazis would later use to seize control of Germany.

stinging from the loss in World War I and its restrictions under the Treaty of Versailles, also reacted favorably to Hitler's ideas of expansion and restoring Germany's honor. Some criticized the new dictator, but his popularity steadily increased. World War I hero General Erich Ludendorff offered an opposing view of Hitler: "I solemnly prophesy . . . that this damnable man will plunge our Reich into the abyss and bring inconceivable misery down upon our nation."[1]

EARLY SUCCESS

Germany prospered economically during the first five years under Hitler, winning him further acceptance among German citizens. Between 1933 and 1937, unemployment in Germany dropped dramatically. At the same time, national income and production both doubled. These changes were partially due to the rebuilding of the country's military, as well as increased public spending on such projects as the Autobahn, a national highway system.

Hitler's early expansions went according to plan. Germany added Austria and the Sudetenland to its territory without firing a shot. On August 23, 1939, the Soviet Union and Germany stunned the world by signing a nonaggression treaty. The treaty enabled Hitler to delay his planned confrontation with the Soviet Union for a few more years.

Launched on September 1, 1939, Germany's invasion of Poland was the first in a string of German successes in Europe. These included the defeat of France in June 1940. By the beginning of 1941, the United Kingdom was the only major world power left opposing Hitler.

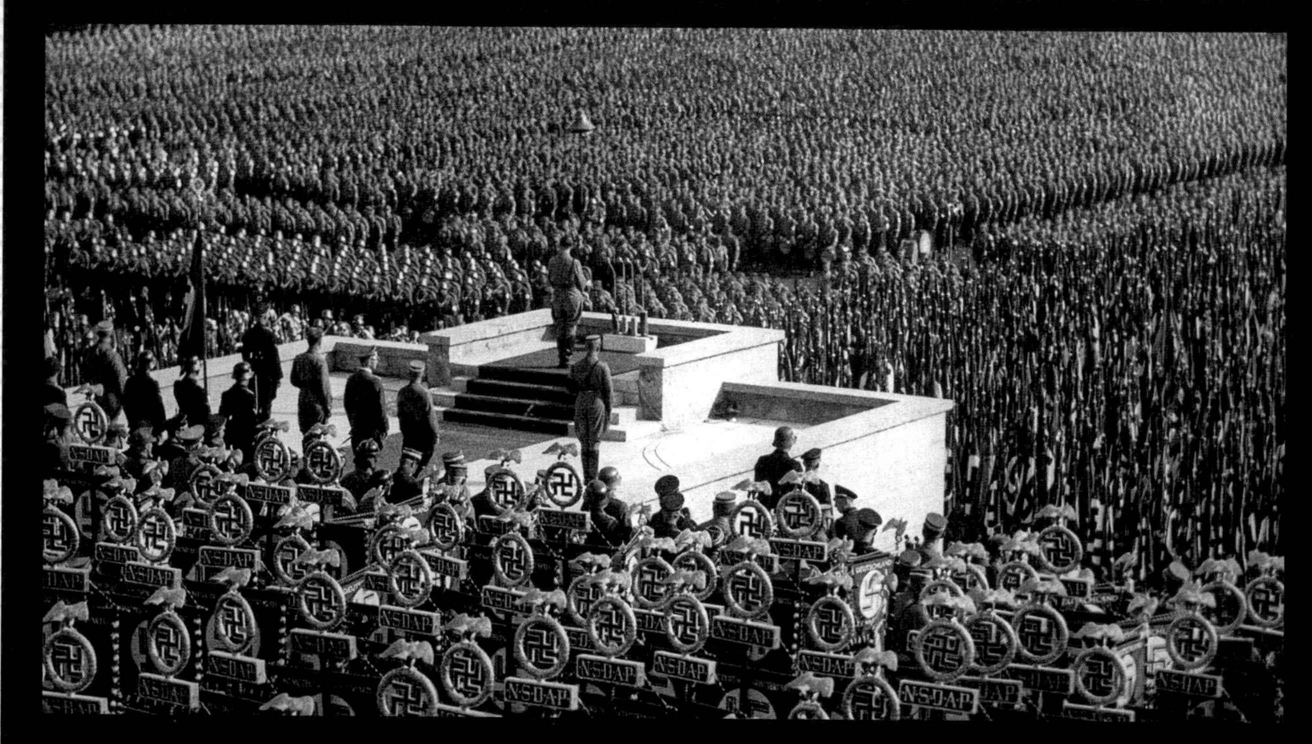

Hitler whipped up support for his vision of Germany at massive rallies.

INVASION OF THE SOVIET UNION

However, Hitler's plans for Lebensraum still called for seizing territory from the Soviet Union, which had become his ally. On June 22, 1941, he broke the nonaggression treaty. More than 3 million troops, 3,600 tanks, and 600,000 motorized vehicles rolled over the Soviet border.[2] Operation Barbarossa, Hitler's invasion of the Soviet Union, had begun.

This was the war Hitler had always wanted—a war to gain living space in the east. The Soviet Union was also rich with natural resources, including oil. Hitler planned to use these resources to fuel the continuing war against the United Kingdom.

Germany was finally at war with an enemy that Nazism had long denounced and trained its citizens to hate. Germany's leaders especially despised the Bolsheviks, a faction of Russian communists that had seized power in the 1917 revolution and created the Soviet Union. Minister of Propaganda Joseph Goebbels summed it up for the public: "Now that the Führer has unmasked the treachery of the Bolshevik rulers, National Socialism, and hence the German people, are reverting to the principles which impelled them—the struggle against plutocracy and Bolshevism."[3]

Initially, huge numbers of German troops, tanks, and planes advanced deep within the Soviet Union, generating hope of a quick victory for the Axis.

JOSEPH GOEBBELS

Joseph Goebbels was the Minister of Propaganda in Germany and one of Hitler's closest aides. He was born in Rheydt, Germany, on October 29, 1897. He joined the Nazi Party in 1924, and within four years he had become one of its most influential members. Two months after Hitler became chancellor in 1933, Goebbels took control of the regime's propaganda. One of his first acts was to arrange a night when books by Jewish or anti-Nazi authors were publicly burned. The burning was held on May 10, 1933. Goebbels controlled every aspect of German cultural and intellectual life. He built up Hitler's image and bombarded the German people with it through the media. As the Allies closed in on Berlin in early May 1945, he poisoned his six children, his wife, and himself.

HITLER'S HOLOCAUST

The Holocaust was Hitler's mass slaughter of Jews and other groups the Nazis believed to be inferior. Approximately 6 million Jews—two-thirds of the total number of Jews in Europe—were persecuted and killed by the Nazis.[4] The Nazis also targeted Poles, Czechs, Greeks, Romani, homosexuals, trade unionists, people with disabilities, and others.

Hitler had long ranted against the Jews. After he became chancellor in 1933, anti-Jewish laws were passed in Germany. Jews were forced out of public life, university and civil service positions, and other areas. Eventually Jews were banned from public schools, theaters, and resorts. Before the war, Hitler claimed that not only would Jews be responsible for any future war, but also that such a war would result in their deaths:

> *Today I will once more be a prophet: if the international Jewish financiers in and outside Europe should succeed in plunging the nations once more into a world war, then the result will not be the Bolshevizing of the earth, and thus the victory of Jewry, but the annihilation of the Jewish race in Europe!*[5]

After Hitler took power, the Nazis built concentration camps to hold Jewish people and others that the regime targeted. Prisoners were forced to work and support the Nazi war effort. Starting in 1941, the Nazis also built another type of camp: death camps. At these places, they sought to carry out what they called the "Final Solution." People were brought like cattle to the camps, herded into gas chambers there, and murdered. Historians estimate the Nazis killed as many as 15 million civilians in the Holocaust.[6]

The Nazis approached within 65 miles (105 km) of Moscow, the country's capital city. Soviet troops were in full retreat. However, the Soviet military regrouped and fought back. The decisive battle was the fight for the city of Stalingrad in the winter of 1942–1943. After the Germans entered the city, a massive Soviet counterattack combined with brutal winter conditions forced the Germans to surrender.

The German army continued suffering losses in 1943, and it was pushed back in North Africa and Italy. In 1944, the Allies' June 6 landing at Normandy, France, and their relentless advance toward Germany made it seem as if it were only a matter of time until Germany was defeated.

ASSASSINATION ATTEMPTS

Hitler survived several assassination attempts during his time as leader of Germany. The attempt that was closest to success came in the summer of 1944. On July 20, Hitler held a military conference at his Eastern Front headquarters near Rastenburg in East Prussia, now part of Poland. The location was known as the Wolfsschanze, or Wolf's Lair. German staff officer Claus von Stauffenberg placed a briefcase with a bomb in it underneath the conference table as the meeting began. He then left the room.

The bomb exploded at approximately 12:45 p.m. Windows and doors blew out of the room, and numerous people were hurt, some critically. Hitler, however, survived. His pants and hair caught fire, he had burns, blisters, wood splinters, cuts, and bruises, and his right arm was swollen and painful, but he was alive. The heavy oak table had protected him from the full force of the

The July 1944 assassination attempt blew the room apart, but Hitler survived.

blast. Hitler had thousands of people arrested and executed in the wake of the attempted assassination.

Though Hitler survived, his armies continued losing ground against the Allies. He launched his last desperate counterattack in December 1944. It became known as the Battle of the Bulge for the way the German forces pushed back the Allied lines in a bulging shape. However, the Allies soon regrouped and repelled the attack. By the third week of April 1945, Soviet troops were closing in on Hitler's bunker in bombed-out and devastated Berlin. Hitler surrounded himself with his closest friends and allies, including his companion, Eva Braun. It was obvious the end for Hitler's Germany was rapidly approaching.

Churchill served in the British government during World War I.

WINSTON CHURCHILL

Winston Churchill was the prime minister of the United Kingdom throughout most of World War II. He was born in a palace on November 30, 1874, in Woodstock, Oxfordshire, England. Churchill entered politics in 1900, winning election to the British Parliament. By 1911 he had become First Lord of the Admiralty, overseeing the United Kingdom's navy.

Churchill's advocacy of the disastrous Gallipoli campaign in Turkey in 1915 during World War I hurt his reputation, and he departed from the government. During the 1930s he repeatedly criticized Germany's growing militarism, and he urged the United Kingdom to build up its own military to meet the challenge.

CHURCHILL AND THE PHONY WAR

When World War II began, it was clear Chamberlain's strategy of giving Hitler what he wanted had failed. Chamberlain had to assemble a war cabinet, and on September 3, Churchill was appointed to it as First Lord of the Admiralty—the same position he had held during World War I. Before his first day was over, Churchill had sent out a blizzard of memos on numerous subjects ranging from the status of German U-boat submarines to how many rifles the British Royal Navy possessed.

In speeches to the British House of Commons and then to the general public, Churchill became the face of the war. "Winston Churchill has emerged from the first five weeks of the war as the most inspiring figure in Great Britain and ultimate successor to the 71-year-old Neville Chamberlain," wrote the *New York Times*.[1]

Churchill was a whirlwind of activity. He ordered that all naval vessels should be equipped with radar and all merchant ships should be armed. He announced how many German U-boats had been sunk. He conceived new war plans, such as sending a naval force into the Baltic Sea and placing mines in Norwegian coastal waters to prevent the transport of iron ore from Sweden to Germany. He went to bed late at night, visiting the war room for more

GALLIPOLI

In World War I, the Ottoman Empire, centered in what is now Turkey, was considered the weak link in the alliance opposing the United Kingdom. Winston Churchill, as Lord of the Admiralty, devised a plan to attack Turkey's Gallipoli peninsula. He expected this would force Germany to deploy troops to help the Ottoman Empire and thus weaken their forces on other fronts. The campaign began in February 1915. The Ottomans fought better than expected, and British efforts were disorganized and chaotic. After almost a year, the British admitted defeat and withdrew. Gallipoli was a British military disaster, and Churchill took the blame.

Churchill's speeches, both in person and broadcast over the radio, made a major impression upon those who listened.

planning rather than sleeping. He credited his incredible energy to his habit of napping for an hour in the afternoon.

The early phase of the war, following the German success in Poland, was dubbed the Phony War. Though they were officially at war with Germany, France and the United Kingdom launched no major offensives. Then the Nazis blasted through Denmark and Norway in April and conquered Holland and Belgium in May. On May 10, 1940, Chamberlain resigned. Churchill succeeded him as prime minister. "I felt as though I were walking with destiny and that all my past life had been a preparation for this hour and this trial," he said.[2]

RALLYING THE NATION

One of Churchill's most important achievements during the early days of his term in office, when it seemed as if the Nazis were unstoppable, was rallying the British people. On June 4, 1940, as German armies swept through Western Europe and it seemed a German invasion of the United Kingdom was coming soon, Churchill gave one of his most memorable speeches. He proclaimed,

> *We shall go on to the end. We shall fight in France, we shall fight on the seas and oceans, we shall fight with growing confidence and growing strength in the air, we shall defend our island, whatever the cost may be. We shall fight on the beaches, we shall fight on the landing grounds, we shall fight in the fields and in the streets, we shall fight in the hills; we shall never surrender.*[3]

France surrendered to Germany on June 25, 1940, leaving the United Kingdom alone against the Nazis. In July, the Luftwaffe began a bombing campaign against the United Kingdom, hoping to soften it up for an invasion

Churchill, *right*, personally surveyed damage in London during the Battle of Britain.

code-named Operation Sea Lion. Throughout July and August, the Luftwaffe and the RAF dueled in the skies over the United Kingdom. The struggle was known as the Battle of Britain. In an August 20 speech, Churchill delivered another iconic phrase in praise of the RAF: “Never in the field of human conflict was so much owed by so many to so few."[4] By mid-September, the German air force had been defeated. Hitler canceled Operation Sea Lion.

THE BLACK DOG

Churchill battled his entire life against depression, which he called his "Black Dog." "I don't like standing near the edge of a platform when an express train is passing through," he once said. "I like to stand right back and if possible get a pillar between me and the train. I don't like to stand by the side of a ship and look down into the water. A second's action would end everything. A few drops of desperation."[5]

Sometimes the depression was associated with specific events, such as when the British army suffered a devastating defeat in Singapore in 1942. It was impossible to predict how long the condition might last. Months after the Singapore defeat, Churchill sat in his bathroom one night wrapped in a towel, staring at the floor. "I cannot get over Singapore," he said sadly.[6] At other times when depression swept over him, it could not be linked to any one thing. His friend Lord Beaverbrook once said Churchill was always very confident or very depressed.

THE CREATIVE CHURCHILL

Churchill was a talented painter and writer. He found solace in painting, particularly during times of strife. He became an accomplished impressionistic landscape artist and produced hundreds of paintings throughout his life. He also painted interior scenes and portraits. As an author, Churchill was extremely prolific. He wrote a six-volume work on World War II and a four-volume work on the history of the United Kingdom, among many other books.

Churchill visited Roosevelt in Washington, DC, after the United States entered the war in December 1941.

CHURCHILL AND ROOSEVELT

When war broke out, even before Churchill was prime minister, Roosevelt invited him to write to him personally, outside of the normal diplomatic channels, about anything he thought important. Churchill took the opportunity. Roosevelt later sent his close aide Harry Hopkins to the United Kingdom to find out what kind of person Churchill was, and the two men took a liking to each other. Hopkins praised Churchill to Roosevelt, also emphasizing that the British needed US help. In March 1941, Roosevelt pushed the Lend-Lease Act through Congress. By the summer, supplies were flowing to the United Kingdom from the still-neutral United States.

In August 1941, the two men had their first face-to-face meeting, and before long were calling each other "Franklin" and "Winston." Attending a religious service with Roosevelt, Churchill burst out crying, feeling a divine power was bringing the two nations together. Churchill knew the United Kingdom needed the United States, and so he went out of his way to

LETTERS BETWEEN FRIENDS

In March 1945, as the war was winding down and Roosevelt's health was fading, Churchill wrote him a letter reminiscing about their cooperation and personal friendship during the war:

> *I hope that the rather numerous telegrams I have to send you on so many of our difficult and intertwined affairs are not becoming a bore to you. Our friendship is the rock on which I build for the future of the world so long as I am one of the builders. I always think of those tremendous days when you devised Lend-Lease, when we met at Argentia, when you decided with my heartfelt agreement to launch the invasion of Africa, and when you comforted me for the loss of Tobruk by giving me the 300 Shermans of subsequent Alamein fame. I remember the part our personal relations have played in the advance of the world cause now nearing its first military goal.*[7]

OPERATION UNTHINKABLE

In early 1945, Churchill secretly authorized the drawing up of plans called Operation Unthinkable that anticipated a war with the Soviet Union. Churchill distrusted Stalin, and the plan assumed the Soviet leader would refuse to honor his Yalta commitments after Germany's defeat. US and British forces would launch a sneak attack on the Soviet army in Germany to force him to do so. The plan was never put into action. Its existence was not made public until the late 1990s.

court Roosevelt's favor. "No man ever wooed a woman as I wooed that man for England," he later said.[8]

After the attack on Pearl Harbor, Churchill established an alliance between the United Kingdom, the United States, and the Soviet Union. These nations, by far the most powerful of the Allies, agreed to defeat Germany first before focusing on Japan. Meetings with Stalin in 1942 and Roosevelt in 1943 laid the groundwork for the opening of a second front in the war against Germany. By 1944, the United States and the United Kingdom would be ready to invade France. The successful invasion led to Germany's defeat in May 1945. Churchill remained prime minister through the end of the war in Europe.

Hirohito, who became emperor at only 25 years old, was among the youngest national leaders of World War II.

HIROHITO

Hirohito, the longest-reigning monarch in Japanese history, was the emperor of Japan during World War II. Hirohito was born Michinomiya Hirohito in a Tokyo palace on April 29, 1901. On December 25, 1926, he became Japan's emperor following the death of his father, Emperor Taisho. Hirohito became his nation's one hundred twenty-fourth emperor. The end of the Taisho Period was proclaimed, and the beginning of the Showa Era, or era of enlightened peace, was announced. As emperor, Hirohito became the commander in chief of Japan's armed forces. In Japan, the emperor was treated like a god. Japanese soldiers were encouraged to become martyrs and sacrifice themselves to honor him. Unlike Roosevelt, who frequently spoke to US citizens on the radio, Hirohito was rarely heard by the Japanese people.

Japan's expansion began in the early 1930s. In 1931, Japan launched an invasion of the Chinese province of Manchuria. Six years later, it began a larger-scale invasion of China. Chinese leader Chiang Kai-Shek, who had been busy fighting a civil war in China, turned his attention to the Japanese invaders. Hundreds of thousands of Japanese troops remained stationed in China throughout World War II, seeking to maintain control of the conquered areas.

AN ASSASSINATION ATTEMPT

On December 27, 1923, Hirohito was on his way to the Diet, the Japanese congress, to deliver a speech. An anarchist named Namba Daisuke ran up to the window of his car and fired a shot at him. Although the bullet shattered the glass and injured an attendant, Hirohito was unharmed. The prime minister and others resigned, and policemen in the area were fired. As a result of the incident, the entire imperial family came under strict guard and could no longer move around freely as they had in the past.

THE TRIPARTITE PACT

Hirohito worked to build up his nation's armed forces as the world moved toward war. In 1939, Japan strengthened its army and constructed new aircraft and ships.

Meanwhile, World War II had begun in Europe. With France and the Netherlands defeated, those nations' resource-rich colonies in Southeast Asia would be open for Japan to seize. For years leading up to World War II, Japan had imported materials it needed, such as petroleum, scrap iron, steel, and copper, from the United States. But Japanese aggression against China led the United States to cut off shipments of critical imports in January 1940. Hirohito recognized such a lack of resources would cripple Japan's military ambitions: "Unless we reduce the size of our army and navy by one-third, we won't make it."[1]

CHIANG KAI-SHEK

1887–1975

Chiang Kai-Shek was the leader of China during World War II. He was born on October 31, 1887, in the town of Xikou, China. He attended military training college in Japan. After returning to China, he participated in a 1911 uprising that established a Chinese republic by overthrowing the Qing Dynasty. He joined the Chinese Nationalist Party, founded by Sun Yat-sen. After Sun's death in 1925, Chiang became head of the party. In 1927, a civil war began between Chiang's Nationalists and the Communists.

In 1937, Japan invaded China, and Chiang aligned his nation with the Allied powers. The Chinese civil war was put on hold until the Japanese could be expelled from China. During the war, Chiang frequently disagreed with his American military adviser, Lieutenant General Joseph Stilwell. Stilwell urged Chiang to better train and equip his troops, but Chiang preferred instead to follow the advice of US Major General Claire Chennault, who felt air power alone could defeat the Japanese. Still, Chiang remained an important ally. In 1943, he attended the Cairo Conference with Roosevelt and Churchill. By the war's end, China had suffered approximately 20 million military and civilian deaths.[2]

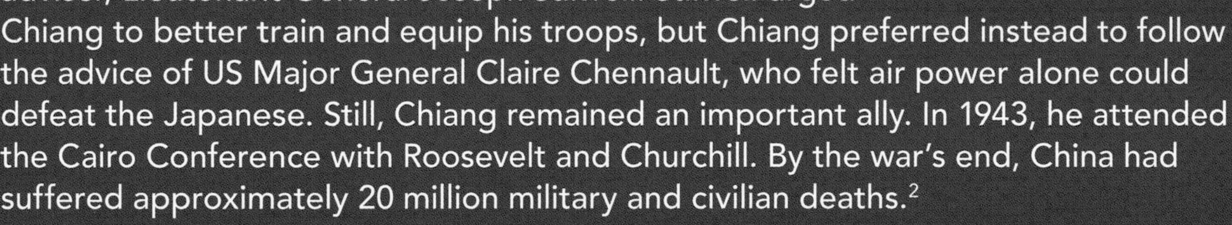

After Japan's defeat, the Chinese civil war resumed. Chiang's Nationalists lost, and the Communist People's Republic of China was established in 1949 under the leadership of Mao Zedong. Chiang relocated his government to the island of Taiwan. He remained president of Taiwan until his death in 1975.

This drove Japan to simultaneously pursue two different foreign policy tracks. First, it sought to reduce tensions with the United States. Second, it sought to strengthen its ties with Germany.

Hitler had been pressing Japan to sign an alliance with Germany and Italy. Such an agreement would commit the Japanese to fight alongside its European allies if any of the three countries went to war against the Soviet Union. Hirohito was reluctant to go along with an alliance, since he knew Japan had not built up its armed forces sufficiently and was not yet ready to fight a large-scale conflict. He agonized over the decision of whether or not to join forces with Nazi Germany. He called the decision the most fateful of his reign and said he could not sleep.

On September 13, 1940, Hirohito studied the wording of the proposed alliance between Germany, Italy, and Japan for hours. Although he knew signing it would likely mean war with the United States, he approved it. On September 27, 1940, Japan officially signed the Tripartite Pact with Italy and Germany. Japan was now firmly committed to the Axis.

PEARL HARBOR

Hirohito's role in the decision to attack the United States naval base at Pearl Harbor in Hawaii on December 7, 1941, is still a matter of debate. According to some historians, on November 5, 1941, the Japanese government made the decision to go to war with the full knowledge of Hirohito. The justification for the war, said a government report, was that the United States and the United Kingdom represented a threat to Japan if they controlled resources in Southeast Asia.

Axis officials in Tokyo toasted the signing of the Tripartite Pact.

However, other historians argue that while Hirohito knew about the planned Pearl Harbor attack, he could do nothing to stop it in the face of Japan's powerful military leaders. In an account Hirohito gave in 1946, he claimed if he had tried to stop the attack, it would have led to his overthrow and possible assassination.

TOJO

Tojo Hideki was Japan's prime minister between 1941 and 1944. For many Americans of the time, he was the Japanese leader most associated with the war, rather than Hirohito. Born on December 30, 1884, in Tokyo, Tojo became vice-minister of war in 1938 and was a leading advocate of the Tripartite Pact. He became minister of war in 1940, and Hirohito selected him as prime minister on October 18, 1941. Under his leadership, Japan initially enjoyed success in the war, but a series of military reversals caused him to resign on July 18, 1944. He was convicted of waging aggressive wars by the Allies and executed by hanging on December 23, 1948.

HIROHITO AT WAR

Despite military successes during the initial phase of the war in 1942, Japan spent much of the following two years slowly retreating from US forces. Hirohito received generals and admirals returning from the war. He encouraged front-line troops. He praised home-front organizations. He visited bases, battleships, and headquarters locations of both the army and navy. He inspected military schools, urged manufacturers to continue production, and followed the latest weapons developments. Still, most ordinary citizens never saw Hirohito or heard his voice, viewing him as a faraway god.

The Japanese naval defeat at the Mariana Islands and its loss in the battle of Saipan in July 1944 caused military leaders to conclude Japan had no hope of winning the war. Yet the country fought on. The following February, Hirohito

Hirohito carried out inspections of Japanese military units during the war.

consulted seven senior leaders about continuing the war. All but one urged him to fight on. Hirohito himself still clung to the hope the war could somehow be won. He wondered if the country would be able to endure continuing hardships until then.

Early in May 1945, Germany surrendered. One option for Japan had been to negotiate for peace before the fall of its powerful ally. Now that opportunity was gone. On May 18, Hirohito's brother Prince Takamatsu suggested Hirohito should abdicate the throne. That would allow him to avoid the humiliation and disgrace of having to surrender to the United States, leaving the job to someone else. Hirohito rejected that idea, and the war continued.

In the last year of the war, the Japanese government had adopted a war policy that used suicide tactics. Pilots known as kamikazes rammed their bomb-filled aircraft and boats into US ships. The Japanese press continued encouraging Japanese citizens to die for Hirohito. However, the emperor knew the war was practically over. On July 12, an adviser told him Japan should surrender. "So be it, then," Hirohito responded.[3]

However, the Japanese did not yet announce a surrender. Outwardly the country appeared committed to fighting to the bitter end. On August 6, the United States dropped an atomic bomb on Hiroshima, killing approximately 80,000 people instantly.[4] Three days later, a second atomic bomb landed on Nagasaki, killing tens of thousands more.[5]

THE CULT OF THE EMPEROR

Under Hirohito's grandfather Meiji the Great, who ruled from the late 1800s until the early 1900s, the monarchy acquired a cult-like status throughout Japan that had not previously existed. The monarchy decreed all Japanese people were the emperor's children. As loyal subjects, they were expected to put hard work and service to the state above personal pleasures or interests. Laws restricted exactly what could be said and written about the emperor. By the time of Hirohito, many Japanese people considered the emperor a god in human form.

On August 15, in a broadcast that represented the first time most Japanese people had heard their emperor's voice, Hirohito announced Japan's surrender. He said in part, "Should we continue to fight it would . . . result in an ultimate collapse and obliteration of the Japanese nation."[6] An estimated 1.5 million Japanese people died between the fall of Saipan, when the war was determined to be unwinnable, and Japan's final surrender.[7]

Stalin, *right*, worked closely with Vladimir Lenin in the years leading up to the creation of the Soviet Union.

JOSEPH STALIN

Joseph Stalin was the leader of the Soviet Union during World War II. He was born Ioseb Besarionis dze Jughashvili on December 18, 1878, in Gori. The city, then a part of Russia, is now within the independent nation of Georgia. Early in his life, Stalin studied for the priesthood, but he was expelled from the seminary in 1899. Around that time, he discovered the writings and philosophy of Vladimir Lenin. Lenin was a socialist revolutionary who followed the teachings of German thinker Karl Marx.

When Lenin formed the Bolshevik political movement in 1903, Stalin joined the organization. His power rose alongside Lenin's as the Bolsheviks took over Russia in 1917. He became general secretary of the Communist Party of the Soviet Union in 1922. When Lenin died in 1924, Stalin emerged victorious from a power struggle among other communist leaders, seizing control of the country. Stalin's harsh economic policies, paranoia, and drive to

LENIN'S TESTAMENT

Stalin might have been removed as a top Communist Party official if Lenin had lived. Evidence is found for this in letters known as "Lenin's Testament," dictated as Lenin recovered from a severe stroke in the winter of 1922–1923. In the document, Lenin wrote that Stalin, having become general secretary of the Communist Party, "has unlimited authority concentrated in his hands, and I am not sure whether he will always be capable of using that authority with sufficient caution." One week later, Lenin called Stalin "too rude."[1] He then proposed removing him as general secretary. However, Lenin died in January 1924 before he could act on his recommendations.

modernize the Soviet Union led to the death of millions of Soviet people in the years before World War II.

THE NONAGGRESSION PACT

The world was shocked when Germany and the Soviet Union signed their nonaggression pact in August 1939. Ever since he wrote *Mein Kampf*, Hitler had made it clear the Soviet Union would be targeted in his nation's expansion for living space.

However, there were several reasons why the pact should not have been a surprise. Since 1935, Stalin had been dropping subtle hints he desired improved relations with Germany. In his speeches, he signaled to Hitler he did not seek to be part of a European war. As a result, Hitler was able to seize Czechoslovakia without fear of provoking the Soviet Union.

Stalin was not ready for a major war in 1939, so the alliance with Germany served his purposes. Although the large Soviet army was well equipped, it lacked

Stalin, *second from right,* signed a nonaggression pact with Germany, delaying a confrontation with Hitler's Nazi regime.

experienced commanders. In 1937 and 1938, Stalin had purged the Soviet military officer corps of those he suspected were disloyal to the country. This included many of its top officers. Within 15 months, 40,000 military officers had been arrested. In the fall of 1938, 13 out of 15 army commanders and 154 out of 195 divisional commanders had been shot on falsified charges.[2] Their replacements lacked battle-tested experience.

For Stalin, another advantage of the nonaggression pact was the secret portion of the agreement concerning Poland. The deal would split a conquered

Poland between Germany and the Soviet Union. The Soviet Union had gone through territorial disputes with Poland, and Stalin looked forward to adding parts of Poland to his nation. Additionally, Poland gave him a buffer zone between the Soviet Union and Germany, leaving German soldiers far from his borders.

STALIN ON THE ATTACK

Germany's blitzkrieg moved with lightning speed across Poland in September 1939. The Germans urged Stalin to attack Poland from the east, but the rapid pace of the German advance surprised Stalin. Before committing his troops, Stalin wanted to know if the Germans would hold to the positions they had secretly agreed upon. Once he received these assurances from Germany, Stalin unleashed his troops on the embattled Poles from the east on September 17. His troops met little resistance. Germany and the Soviet Union now completely controlled Poland.

The territories Stalin took over early in the war experienced what it meant to be under Stalin's thumb. Political, economic, and cultural leaders were rounded up. Some were shot, and some were sent to Siberia, the vast frozen expanse in the east of the Soviet Union. Entire families were deported. Stalin pressured neighboring countries to sign mutual assistance treaties that forced them to allow Soviet troops in their territory.

However, Finland refused. The Soviet Union invaded it on November 30, 1939. Although the Finns fought fiercely, Finland's government realized it could never completely defeat the much larger Soviet army. The two nations signed a peace treaty in March 1940.

Still, Stalin was furious. The Soviet Union had expected to easily crush Finland, but the brief war had exposed weaknesses in the Soviet military. To make matters worse, the quick German defeat of France a few months later meant Hitler no longer had to worry about a war in Western Europe. He could turn his attention to the Soviet Union whenever he wanted. Stalin felt the Soviets needed until 1943 to prepare for a war against Germany. As midsummer of 1941 approached, Stalin ignored evidence the Germans were moving men and weapons to his borders. When Georgy Zhukov, one of his top generals, tried to get him to see the reality of the situation, Stalin angrily scolded him.

THE KATYN FOREST MASSACRE

In the Katyn Forest Massacre, Stalin ordered the killing of more than 20,000 Poles who were deemed foes of Communism and Soviet rule.[3] After Stalin took over his portion of Poland in September 1939, his police forces rounded up Poles and sent them to interrogation centers. In April and May 1940, the prisoners were taken to three execution areas and murdered. German troops discovered the mass burial ground at Katyn Forest in the Soviet Union in 1943, causing international outrage. The Soviet Union claimed the Nazis had carried out the killings. It only admitted Stalin was responsible in 1990.

OPERATION BARBAROSSA

At 3:40 a.m. on the morning of June 22, 1941, Stalin was awakened by a telephone call from Zhukov informing him German troops had surged across the Soviet border. The Soviet Union was now at war with Germany.

For years, historians' accepted version of the events immediately following the invasion was taken from the account of future Soviet leader Nikita Khrushchev. He wrote the attack completely unnerved Stalin and led him to announce he was giving up his leadership. For the next week or so, Khrushchev said, Stalin was demoralized and stayed in his home, leaving the Soviet Union leaderless as German troops raced across Soviet territory.

However, another version of events emerged in the 1990s, taken from the records of Stalin's office. It showed Stalin in full control, issuing orders to meet the Nazi threat in the days following the invasion. Stalin and his military commanders miscalculated by figuring the main thrust of the Nazi assault was heading toward the Ukraine, an area rich in raw materials including grain, coal, and oil. They sent much of the Soviet army there.

The Germans were actually heading toward Moscow, the Soviet capital city. However, the German advance stalled outside of Moscow, and then the harsh Soviet winter began. The cold disabled German vehicles and killed German soldiers.

When spring 1942 came, the Germans shifted focus and headed toward Stalingrad. Again they had early successes. On July 28, 1942, Stalin issued Order No. 227 to the troops defending the city, telling them not to take a step backward. The order labeled retreat as treason and said those caught retreating were to be shot on the spot. The Soviet resistance stiffened. Then the brutal Soviet winter set in again, preventing supplies from reaching the German forces. Eventually German troops were reduced to chewing tree bark for food. By the time the German units at Stalingrad surrendered on February 2, 1943, approximately 250,000 Axis troops were dead.[4] After the victory, the Soviets seized the momentum and began steadily pushing back the Germans.

As German forces moved through the Soviet Union, they demolished statues of Stalin.

YALTA

The D-Day invasion of June 6, 1944, represented the opening of the second front Stalin had long requested. The Allied troops pouring into France took pressure off Soviet troops in the East, and Stalin's response was enthusiastic: "Military history knows no other enterprise comparable in its breadth of conception, the grandeur of its dimensions and the mastery of its execution."[5]

By the time the Big Three met at Yalta in early February 1945, it was clear Germany would soon be defeated. Stalin's goal at Yalta was to establish a buffer zone between the Soviet Union and Western Europe. He also wanted to be rewarded for agreeing to enter the war against Japan after Germany was defeated, as well as to receive financial repayment for Soviet war expenditures. Stalin was a realistic negotiator who knew what he wanted. In the end, Stalin got his buffer countries. Though the communist Soviet Union and democratic United States were still allies, it was becoming clear the tensions in their relationship could make them enemies in the postwar world.

MAN OF THE YEAR

Joseph Stalin was named Man of the Year by *Time* magazine twice, in 1939 and 1942. In 1939 he was recognized for the German-Soviet nonaggression pact, which transformed Europe. In 1942 *Time* wrote about Stalin's wartime resolve: "The year 1942 was a year of blood and strength. The man whose name means steel in Russian, whose few words of English include the American expression 'tough guy' was the man of 1942. Only Joseph Stalin fully knew how close Russia stood to defeat in 1942, and only Joseph Stalin fully knew how he brought Russia through."[6]

Soviet diplomats and generals accompanied Stalin at the Yalta Conference.

De Gaulle, *left*, fought against Germany during World War I.

CHARLES DE GAULLE

Charles André Joseph Pierre Marie de Gaulle was born on November 22, 1890, in Lille, France. He decided upon a military career and spent four years at the prestigious French Military Academy Saint-Cyr. Because he was tall and thin, with a high forehead and large nose, he was nicknamed "the great asparagus" at the academy.[1] De Gaulle went on to see action during World War I, during which he was wounded several times and became a German prisoner of war.

FRANCE DEFEATED

De Gaulle remained in the French army between the wars. During the Czechoslovakia crisis of 1938, when war with Germany seemed imminent, France was in a panic. Chamberlain and French Premier Edouard Daladier negotiated the Munich Agreement with Hitler, giving the German dictator Czechoslovakia. Although many French people celebrated the agreement because it prevented war, de Gaulle warned it was a temporary solution.

He compared the situation to an incident during the French Revolution of the late 1700s, in which a woman on her way to be executed begged for a delay: "Thanks to today's capitulation we will gain a short breathing space, like the old Madame du Barry begging on the revolutionary scaffold 'A little moment more, Mr. Executioner!'"[2]

When Hitler invaded Poland in 1939, the United Kingdom and France declared war on Germany in response. During the Phony War, while Western Europe was quiet, the French military command waited for Hitler to act. Many French leaders were confident the German army would repeat what it had done in World War I: attack France through Belgium. De Gaulle was one of the few who realized the new German army was different than before, but his words were ignored.

On April 8, 1940, the Phony War ended as the German blitzkrieg stormed into Denmark, followed by Norway. Within a few weeks the Germans had routed the French at the battle of Sedan and were rolling through France from the east. De Gaulle's tank command achieved one of the few French successes against the Germans, and he was promoted to the rank of brigadier general. However, it was too late to save France. Learning on June 16 that the new French prime minister, World War I hero Marshall Philippe Pétain, was planning on surrendering to Germany, de Gaulle refused to accept defeat and flew to London the next day. There he became the exiled head of the Free French, a resistance movement.

De Gaulle continued serving as the military leader of the Free French while living in the United Kingdom.

THE FREE FRENCH

On June 18, de Gaulle delivered a four-minute radio address in which he identified himself as head of the Free French movement and urged the French people to resist the Pétain government, known as Vichy France after the town in which it was located. In response, the German-controlled Vichy government condemned de Gaulle to death for treason.

Free French recruitment was slow at first. The United States officially recognized Vichy France, and only the United Kingdom regarded de Gaulle as legitimate. By mid-August 1940, the Free French army numbered just 2,250 men.[3]

Within four months the numbers had jumped to 17,500 men, resulting from a tour de Gaulle made of France's African colonies.[4] Wherever he went, he was greeted with flag-waving crowds, leading de Gaulle to proclaim enthusiastically, "I am France."[5] Decrees from his London headquarters now were issued with a special phrase: "In the name of the French Empire, we, General de Gaulle, chief of the Free France."[6]

Once Germany declared war on the United States in December 1941, de Gaulle realized Germany had made a mistake and would eventually lose the war. From then on he concentrated on positioning France in the postwar world so it could regain its empire and be considered a great power once again.

MOVE TO ALGIERS

On May 30, 1943, de Gaulle moved his headquarters from London to Algiers, an African portion of the French empire not under Nazi control, so that he could

Giraud, *left*, and de Gaulle struggled for power leading up to the liberation of France.

work on French soil. Initially he shared power as head of the French Committee of National Liberation (FCNL) with Henri Giraud, who was the United States' preferred candidate for FCNL head. However, Giraud made a critical error when he left for the United States in early July on a trip that was supposed to demonstrate US support for him. By the time Giraud returned to Algiers in late July, de Gaulle was firmly in charge, and soon he became the sole head of the FCNL.

Despite de Gaulle's position, neither the United States nor the Soviet Union viewed him favorably when the Big Three met at Tehran in 1943. Stalin saw de Gaulle as representing an imaginary France; he believed the real one had sided with the Vichy government. He felt the country should be punished for aiding the Axis and should not get its colonies back after the war. Roosevelt agreed. Only Churchill spoke in support of France.

As D-Day approached in June 1944, the administration of France after its liberation was a major issue. Roosevelt disliked and distrusted de Gaulle, and he did not want the FCNL to take over France. He favored a military occupation of France until the people were free to choose their government. De Gaulle was afraid that once the Vichy government collapsed and the Nazis left, there would be a power vacuum the communists would try to fill. He said he would not stand for another authoritarian government. Churchill invited de Gaulle to England to try to resolve the question, but the meeting became heated. "Why do you seem to

SABOTAGE

On April 21, 1943, de Gaulle was set to fly to Scotland to inspect the Free French Navy. However, a key component of the aircraft had been melted with acid, causing the vehicle's tail to drop after takeoff and nearly resulting in a crash. It was a clear case of sabotage, but no one was ever arrested for the incident. It did, however, increase de Gaulle's mistrust of the United States and the United Kingdom.

think that I need to put before Roosevelt my candidacy for authority in France?" de Gaulle asked.[7] Churchill replied that it was because of the United States that France was to be liberated. He got so mad at de Gaulle that he threatened to send him back to Algiers in chains.

Eventually it became clear the French people would accept de Gaulle as their leader. Bayeux was the first town de Gaulle visited when he returned to France on June 14, and he was greeted by a cheering, weeping mob of people. He soon found this was the type of reception he would receive throughout his home country.

GUNFIRE CELEBRATION

When de Gaulle first returned to Paris on August 26 and appeared before the people, he went to Notre Dame Cathedral. As he exited the car, a gun battle broke out between opponents and supporters of the disgraced Vichy government. De Gaulle's aides tried to get him to take cover, but he shrugged them away and walked straight into the church while bullets whizzed around him.

LEADER OF THE PROVISIONAL FRENCH GOVERNMENT

On August 26, 1944, de Gaulle appeared in Paris at the monument known as the Arc de Triomphe to a crowd of adoring thousands. Ever since childhood, he had dreamed of serving France. Now the dream was fulfilled. "I feel not a person but an instrument of Destiny," he said of that moment.[8]

On September 10, 1944, the Provisional Government of the French Republic formed with de Gaulle at its head. As leader of a recently occupied country, de Gaulle faced numerous immediate problems. Public services were not operational. Food, fuel, and electricity were scarce. A quarter of all housing had

Huge crowds cheered de Gaulle's return to Paris.

been destroyed. There was also the problem of what to do with the resistance movement and the communists, which had both fought the Germans during the occupation and expected some sort of inclusion in the new government as a reward.

It would not be an easy time. De Gaulle's differences with the Americans and British had made him many enemies. This included Churchill, who believed de Gaulle harbored a strong dislike of the United Kingdom. He called de Gaulle "one of the greatest dangers to European peace." Churchill said, "in the long run no understanding will be reached with General de Gaulle."[9]

IMAGINING DE GAULLE AT YALTA

History might have taken a different course if de Gaulle had been invited to the Yalta conference, where Roosevelt, Stalin, and Churchill decided the fate of Europe. Some historians argue the ill Roosevelt was unable to stand up to Stalin's demands regarding Eastern Europe. De Gaulle later claimed that if he had been invited to the conference, he would have been able to resist Stalin and represent Western interests better than Roosevelt did.

Japan's surrender documents were signed on the deck of the battleship USS *Missouri*.

THE FINAL BATTLE

World War II ended in Europe on May 7, 1945, when Germany surrendered to the Allies. The war in the Pacific ended several months later, on September 2, 1945, with Japan's surrender. Some of the major powers' national and military leaders survived the conflict to its end. Others did not.

LEADERS WHO DID NOT SURVIVE THE WAR

On March 30, 1945, Roosevelt arrived at Warm Springs, Georgia, for rest and relaxation. At first he was so tired that all he could do was sit in a chair with a book in his hands. However, in the following days, he seemed to recover. In the early afternoon of April 12, he was having his portrait painted by artist Elizabeth Shoumatoff. Suddenly he said, "I have a terrific headache," and slumped forward in his chair.[1] He had suffered a cerebral hemorrhage. Roosevelt was pronounced dead.

In mid-April, 1945, Mussolini was in Milan, Italy. With Allied forces closing in, Mussolini, his mistress, and several others attempted to escape to the Swiss border. There, they hoped they could sneak or fight their way into the neutral country. Mussolini put on a German military coat and helmet as a disguise and joined a group of German soldiers. However, a group of communists attacked them, and Mussolini was discovered. On April 28, the communists executed Mussolini, his mistress, and most of the others. Mussolini's body was defaced by a mob, then taken to a gas station and hung upside down.

Hitler had remained in his Berlin bunker since mid-January 1945, as Allied troops marched toward Berlin. In late April, with Soviet gunfire ringing out just blocks away, Hitler knew the end had come. On April 29, he married his longtime companion, Eva Braun. On April 30, Hitler and Braun committed suicide. Aware of Mussolini's fate, Hitler had ordered the bunker staff to take their bodies outside, douse them in gasoline, and set them ablaze.

HARRY S. TRUMAN

Vice President Harry S. Truman succeeded Roosevelt as president of the United States. Born on May 8, 1884, in Lamar, Missouri, Truman became a US senator in 1935. In 1944, Roosevelt selected him to replace current vice president Henry Wallace on the presidential ticket. Truman guided the country through the end of the war against Germany and Japan. He made the final decision to use atomic bombs in the closing stages of the war in the Pacific. In 1948, Truman won the presidential election, beating Thomas E. Dewey in a historic upset.

POSTWAR LEADERS

Stalin lived to see the war end in both Europe and Asia. After the war, he established communist regimes in many central and European countries, including East Germany, Poland, and Hungary. He died of a cerebral hemorrhage on March 5, 1953, at age 74. In the years after his death, many of his killings and purges were brought to light in the Soviet Union. Later leaders launched a program known as de-Stalinization, deconstructing the cult of personality Stalin had built around himself.

Churchill lived to see Germany defeated and the war in Europe end. But in July 1945, he was unexpectedly defeated for reelection. Clement Attlee became the British prime minister. In 1951, Churchill again was elected prime

Mussolini's gruesome fate may have encouraged Hitler to commit suicide to avoid ending up the same way.

minister. He held that position until he resigned in 1955 for health reasons. He died on January 24, 1965, at the age of 90.

De Gaulle helped rebuild France after the war and retired in 1946. However, he returned in 1958 to lead France as its president. He repaired his relationship with Churchill and served as president until April 1969, when he retired for good. He died on November 9, 1970, at age 79.

Of the World War II leaders, Hirohito lived the longest. After Japan's surrender, US general Douglas MacArthur ran the country. He decided to keep Hirohito on the throne, rather than prosecuting him for war crimes. MacArthur believed the emperor could become a symbol of unity and comfort to the Japanese people as they rebuilt their country. Hirohito survived until January 7, 1989, living to see Japan become a dominant economic power in Asia and the world.

POTSDAM CONFERENCE

The Potsdam Conference, held in occupied Germany from mid-July to early August 1945, concerned the postwar peace in Europe. In attendance were a new Big Three: Stalin, new US president Harry S. Truman, and new British prime minister Clement Atlee. It was agreed at Potsdam to divide Germany into four occupation zones of Allied and Soviet influence. The conference also laid out the surrender terms for Japan.

A POSTWAR WORLD

The actions of national leaders during World War II had effects that lasted decades. Hitler's destruction of Germany led postwar German leaders to ban Nazism and other extremist political parties. In Japan, the ruinous effects of the war inspired the nation to legally renounce war as a means of solving conflicts. Allied occupations and assistance, planned

DOUGLAS MACARTHUR

1880–1964

Douglas MacArthur was born on January 26, 1880, in Little Rock, Arkansas. He graduated at the top of his class at the US Military Academy at West Point in 1903. He led a stubborn defense of the Philippines before they fell to the Japanese in early 1942. When he retreated from the Philippines he vowed to return.

MacArthur's triumphant return came in October 1944, as US forces defeated the Japanese in the Philippines. In 1945, he was appointed commander of all US Army forces in the Pacific. He accepted the formal Japanese surrender on September 2, 1945. After the war he served as Allied commander of the Japanese occupation. He and his staff created Japan's new constitution, initiating reforms in women's rights, land distribution, education, and other areas.

MacArthur later commanded US forces in the Korean War (1950–1953). President Truman removed him from command after he felt MacArthur was disrespecting the president's ultimate military authority. MacArthur died in 1964.

and established by Roosevelt and Truman, helped stabilize and rebuild Germany and Japan. By the late 1900s, both nations had become economically prosperous.

Stalin's establishment of communist regimes in Eastern Europe set the stage for the Cold War, an ideological conflict between the democratic United States and the communist Soviet Union. Though the two nations never fought directly, the Korean War and the Vietnam War (1955–1973) both pitted democratic forces with US support against communist forces with Soviet support. The Cold War was one of the key factors in global politics in the late 1900s.

Separated from the war's battlefields by two oceans, the United States emerged from World War II as the most powerful nation in the world. With Truman and later presidents steering it into the postwar era, it built on this advantage. Its economy and military spending dwarfed those of most other countries. US dominance of world politics continued through the end of the 1900s and into the 2000s. Though the leaders who guided the nations of World War II during the conflict died decades ago, echoes of their actions are still being felt in the modern world.

THE UNITED NATIONS

Creating the United Nations (UN) was a goal of President Franklin D. Roosevelt. This international organization was seen as a replacement for the ineffective League of Nations established after World War I. Based in New York City, the UN had 51 member countries at its birth. It was designed to promote international cooperation and prevent another global conflict. By 2015, the UN was composed of 193 members representing nearly the entire population of Earth.

1933
Adolf Hitler becomes chancellor of Germany; his Nazi Party takes power.

1939
One August 23, the Soviet Union and Germany sign a nonaggression pact.

1940
Winston Churchill becomes leader of the British government on May 10.

1940
Germany, Italy, and Japan sign the Tripartite Pact on September 22, creating the Axis alliance.

1945
President Roosevelt dies on April 12 and is succeeded by Harry S. Truman.

1945
Mussolini is executed on April 28.

1945
Hitler commits suicide on April 30 as Soviet troops close in on him.

1945
Japan surrenders to US General Douglass MacArthur and the Allies on September 2.

ESSENTIAL FACTS

KEY PLAYERS

- Winston Churchill serves as prime minister of the United Kingdom.
- Joseph Stalin leads the Soviet Union through the war.
- Franklin D. Roosevelt is president of the United States.
- Benito Mussolini is the dictator of Italy.
- Adolf Hitler is the dictator of Germany.
- Hirohito is the emperor of Japan.
- De Gaulle is a French leader during the Nazi occupation of his country.

KEY STATISTICS

- More than 3 million German troops were used in the invasion of Russia in 1941.
- Stalin had 40,000 military officers arrested in his purges.
- De Gaulle's Free French army numbered just 2,250 men in August 1940.
- Nazi Germany killed approximately 6 million Jewish people in the Holocaust.

KEY ALLIANCES

- Germany and the Soviet Union signed a nonaggression treaty in August 1939.
- Germany, Italy, and Japan signed the Tripartite Pact in September 1940.
- Roosevelt launched the Lend-Lease program in December 1940, providing military assistance to the United Kingdom and other Allied nations while still keeping the United States technically neutral.

IMPACT ON THE WAR

The personalities and politics of national leaders during World War II had a significant influence on the war. Adolf Hitler's persuasive speaking style and blitzkrieg tactics won him massive support from the German people. His later paranoia and poor military decisions led to Germany's defeat. Roosevelt's connection with Churchill led to US military support for the United Kingdom. Churchill's dramatic speeches and his resolve in the face of German bombing helped inspire the British people to continue their struggle.

QUOTE

"I felt as though I were walking with destiny and that all my past life had been a preparation for this hour and this trial."

—*Winston Churchill*

GLOSSARY

ABDICATE
To step down as a monarch.

ARSENAL
A supply of weapons.

CASUALTY
A person who is injured, missing, or killed during a military campaign.

COUP
An attempt to overthrow leaders.

DENOUNCE
To condemn.

FASCIST
A government having a powerful leader that puts the needs of the country over the freedoms of individual citizens.

ISOLATIONIST
A person who believes his or her country should avoid international conflicts.

NATIONALIST
A person who believes his or her own country is superior to others.

PROPAGANDA
Information that carries facts or details slanted to favor a single point of view or political bias.

RELENTLESS
Not giving up.

SOCIALIST
A person who believes the economy should be controlled by communities or countries, rather than by the decisions of individuals.

SOLACE
Comfort.

ADDITIONAL RESOURCES

SELECTED BIBLIOGRAPHY

Johnson, Paul. *Churchill*. New York: Viking, 2009. Print.

Service, Robert. *Stalin*. Cambridge, MA: Belknap, 2004. Print.

Wilson, A. N. *Hitler*. New York: Basic, 2012. Print.

FURTHER READINGS

Adams, Simon. *World War II*. New York: DK, 2014. Print.

Hamen, Susan E. *World War II*. Minneapolis, MN: Abdo, 2014. Print.

Kesselring, Mari. *How to Analyze the Works of Franklin D. Roosevelt*. Minneapolis, MN: Abdo, 2013. Print.

Vander Hook, Sue. *Adolf Hitler: German Dictator*. Minneapolis, MN: Abdo, 2011. Print.

WEBSITES

To learn more about Essential Library of World War II, visit **booklinks.abdopublishing.com**. These links are routinely monitored and updated to provide the most current information available.

PLACES TO VISIT

FDR Home and Library
4097 Albany Post Road
Hyde Park, NY 12538
1-800-FDR-VISIT
http://www.nps.gov/hofr/index.htm
The home of Franklin D. Roosevelt is preserved as a museum dedicated to Roosevelt's legacy. The museum preserves items related to the lives of the Roosevelts, including during the wartime years.

The National World War II Museum
945 Magazine Street
New Orleans, LA 70130
504-528-1944
http://www.nationalww2museum.org
This museum has been designated by the US Congress as the official US museum of World War II. Its collection features not just weapons and vehicles, but also personal items from people involved in the war, such as photos, letters, and artwork.

SOURCE NOTES

CHAPTER 1. THE WORLD IN FLAMES

1. A. N. Wilson. *Hitler.* New York: Basic, 2012. Print. 41.

2. Ibid. 42.

3. "The Beer Hall Putsch." *History Learning Site.* History Learning Site, 2015. Web. 27 Mar. 2015.

4. "Beer Hall Putsch." *Holocaust Encyclopedia.* United States Holocaust Memorial Museum, 20 June 2014. Web. 1 Apr. 2015.

5. "Beer Hall Putsch." *History Channel.* History Channel, 2015. Web. 27 Mar. 2015.

6. "Treaty of Versailles." *Holocaust Encyclopedia.* United States Holocaust Memorial Museum, 20 June 2014. Web. 1 Apr. 2015.

7. A. J. P. Taylor. *The Origins of the Second World War.* New York: Atheneum, 1962. Print. 186.

8. Conrad Black. *Franklin Delano Roosevelt—Champion of Freedom.* New York: Perseus, 2003. Print. 685.

CHAPTER 2. FRANKLIN D. ROOSEVELT

1. Ted Morgan. *FDR—A Biography.* New York: Simon, 1985. Print. 574.

2. Ibid. 575.

3. Roy Jenkins. *Franklin Delano Roosevelt.* New York: Holt, 2003. Print. 129.

4. Ted Morgan. *FDR—A Biography.* New York: Simon, 1985. Print. 632.

5. Robert Nisbet. *Roosevelt and Stalin—The Failed Courtship.* Washington, DC: Regnery Gateway, 1988. Print. 6.

CHAPTER 3. BENITO MUSSOLINI

1. Dennis Mack Smith. *Mussolini.* New York: Knopf, 1982. Print. 173.

2. R. J. B. Bosworth. *Mussolini.* London: Arnold, 2002. Print. 317.

3. Ibid. 211.

4. Ibid. 356.

5. Dennis Mack Smith. *Mussolini.* New York: Knopf, 1982. Print. 236.

6. R. J. B. Bosworth. *Mussolini.* London: Arnold, 2002. Print. 369.

CHAPTER 4. ADOLF HITLER

1. A. N. Wilson. *Hitler*. New York: Basic, 2012. Print. 85.

2. Ian Kershaw. *Hitler*. New York: Norton, 2000. Print. 393.

3. John Toland. *Adolf Hitler*. New York: Ballantine, 1976. Print. 922.

4. Steve Paulsson. "A View of the Holocaust." *BBC History*. BBC, 17 Feb. 2011. Web. 27 Mar. 2015.

5. Michael Burleigh. *The Racial State*. Cambridge, MA: Cambridge UP, 1991. Print. 199.

6. Steve Paulsson. "A View of the Holocaust." *BBC History*. BBC, 17 Feb. 2011. Web. 27 Mar. 2015.

CHAPTER 5. WINSTON CHURCHILL

1. Paul Addison. *Churchill—The Unexpected Hero*. Oxford, UK: Oxford UP, 2005. Print. 157.

2. Ibid. 161.

3. Carlo D'Este. *Warlord—A Life of Winston Churchill at War*. New York: HarperCollins, 2008. Print. 433.

4. Paul Johnson. *Churchill*. Detroit, MI: Thorndike, 2009. Print. 160.

5. Sarah Freeman. "Winston Churchill and Manic Depression." *Bipolar Lives*. Bipolar Lives, 2015. Web. 27 Mar. 2015.

6. Carlo D'Este. *Warlord—A Life of Winston Churchill at War*. New York: HarperCollins, 2008. Print. 569.

7. Edwin McDowell. "Roosevelt-Churchill Letters Depict Tension." *New York Times*. New York Times, 11 July 1984. Web. 27 Mar. 2015.

8. Carlo D'Este. *Warlord—A Life of Winston Churchill at War*. New York: HarperCollins, 2008. Print. 497.

SOURCE NOTES
CONTINUED

CHAPTER 6. HIROHITO

1. Herbert P. Bix. *Hirohito and the Making of Modern Japan*. New York: Perennial, 2000. Print. 353.

2. "By the Numbers: World-Wide Deaths." *National World War II Museum*. National World War II Museum, n.d. Web. 1 Apr. 2015.

3. David Bergamini. *Japan's Imperial Conspiracy*. New York: William Morrow, 1971. Print. 77.

4. "Fact File: Hiroshima and Nagasaki." *WW2 People's War*. BBC, n.d. Web. 1 Apr. 2015.

5. Ibid.

6. David Bergamini. *Japan's Imperial Conspiracy*. New York: William Morrow, 1971. Print.112.

7. Daikichi Irokawa. *The Age of Hirohito*. New York: Free Press, 1995. Print. 30.

CHAPTER 7. JOSEPH STALIN

1. "Letter to the Congress." *Marxists.org*. Marxists.org, n.d. Web. 27 Mar. 2015.

2. Roy Medvedev and Zhores Medvedev. *The Unknown Stalin*. Woodstock, NY: Overlook, 2004. Print. 235.

3. "Katyn Massacre." *Encyclopaedia Britannica*. Encyclopaedia Britannica, 2015. Web. 1 Apr. 2015.

4. "Battle of Stalingrad." *Encyclopaedia Britannica*. Encyclopaedia Britannica, 2015. Web. 1 Apr. 2015.

5. Ronald Hingley. *Joseph Stalin: Man and Legend*. New York: McGraw-Hill, 1974. Print. 352.

6. "Joseph Stalin Is Named Time Magazine's 'Person Of The Year' For A Second Time." *World History Project*. World History Project, 2015. Web. 27 Mar. 2015.

CHAPTER 8. CHARLES DE GAULLE

1. "Charles De Gaulle." *World Heritage Encyclopedia.* World Heritage Encyclopedia, n.d. Web. 27 Mar. 2015.

2. Jonathan Fenby. *The General—Charles De Gaulle and the France He Saved.* New York: Skyhorse, 2012. Print. 115.

3. Charles Williams. *The Last Great Frenchman—A Life of General De Gaulle.* New York: Wiley, 1993. Print. 125.

4. Ibid. 125.

5. Ibid. 137.

6. Jonathan Fenby. *The General—Charles De Gaulle and the France He Saved.* New York: Skyhorse, 2012. Print. 157.

7. Charles Williams. *The Last Great Frenchman—A Life of General De Gaulle.* New York: Wiley, 1993. Print. 252.

8. Bernard Ledwidge. *De Gaulle.* New York: Saint Martin's, 1982. Print. 181.

9. Ibid. 201.

CHAPTER 9. THE FINAL BATTLE

1. Ted Morgan. *FDR—A Biography.* New York: Simon, 1985. Print. 763.

INDEX

ABOUT THE AUTHOR

Russell Roberts is an award-winning fulltime freelance writer who has published more than 60 books for both children and adults, including the regional best seller *Down the Jersey Shore* and *10 Days to a Sharper Memory.* Among his dozens of children's books are examinations of the lives of Thomas Jefferson, Alexander Hamilton, Robert Goddard, Philo T. Farnsworth, Alicia Keys, Galileo, and Nostradamus, as well as volumes about the Statue of Liberty, Abraham Lincoln and the abolition of slavery, and life in ancient China.